PSALMS
REDUX

Poems and Prayers

Every blessing,
Carla

PSALMS
REDUX

POEMS AND PRAYERS

Carla A. Grosch-Miller

CANTERBURY
PRESS
Norwich

Copyright in this volume © Carla A. Grosch-Miller 2014

First published in 2014 by the Canterbury Press Norwich
Editorial office
3rd Floor, Invicta House
108–114 Golden Lane
London EC1Y OTG

Canterbury Press is an imprint of Hymns Ancient & Modern
Ltd (a registered charity)
13A Hellesdon Park Road, Norwich,
Norfolk NR6 5DR, UK

www.canterburypress.co.uk

British Library Cataloguing in Publication data

A catalogue record for this book is available
from the British Library

978 1 84825 639 2

Typeset by Manila Typesetting Company
Printed and bound in Great Britain by
CPI Group (UK) Ltd, Croydon

Contents

INTRODUCTION

This project began out of the blue when, after a number of years of sporadic attempts at daily prayer, I resolved at the start of 2012 to use every day a prayer book I had been using on and off since 1998, *A Guide to Prayer for All God's People*.[1] This treasured book contains daily scripture readings, other devotional offerings, a hymn and, most importantly for this project, a weekly psalm.

The first week I stumbled over the psalm. The metaphors used and structures of belief underpinning the idea of God simply did not relate to my faith. Whilst the original words had a beauty and resonance that came from the wisdom of the early writer and my own deep familiarity with the text, I could not pray that first psalm (and some others after that) at depth and with integrity. So I rewrote it and christened it a *Psalm redux*, the 'redux' signifying that it was a restoration and refreshment of the ancient text.

From that time on, I found the writing of a weekly psalm redux to be part of my prayer discipline, sometimes hesitantly (reluctant to disturb ancient texts so beautiful and meaningful), other times of necessity. A few of the psalms reflect the wrestling that accompanies the emergence of new understandings of the God who gives us life and invites us to flourish.

---

1 Job, R.P. and Shawchuck, N., 1989, Nashville: Upper Room Books.

Psalms redux are not meant to supplant the psalms that are the foundation and poetry of our faith. Rather they are prayer aids for those of us who need a fresh language that guides us into the depths of renewing prayer. Most are geared to the individual at prayer; some are easily used in corporate worship.

I offer these to you with the prayer that they will refresh your prayer life and guide you into the depths, as they have for me.

Carla A. Grosch-Miller
Oxford 2013

Delight is born of discipline chosen.
Contentment grows with wisdom.
Deep listening leads
along a cairn-marked trail,
dew clinging to grass bent
by pilgrim feet.

The sky is blue here.
Birdsong lifts the head.
A cool breeze caresses the cheek.
Legs grow strong like tree trunks;
arms branch flexibly
and dance with the wind.
From each finger drips
a ripening fruit.

The water is fresh and clear.
The plain is broad.
Come.

Psalm 3 *redux*

The sins of religion have gone public:
   rigidity, hypocrisy, intolerance, wilful ignorance
     and worse –
   the crushing of the spirit of those whom God
     cherishes,
   the dealing of death to those whose life is precious.
In response, many are faith's foes.
Talk of the Holy is met with distain and mockery.

But You, O God, continue to re-create the world,
   dancing at the fragile edge,
   breathing at the margins,
   in vulnerability offering Yourself
     again and again.

You call us into quiet, into a nurturing beyond words.
You strengthen our backs and stretch our hearts.
You lift our heads and spur our songs.
You move in and beyond us,
   inviting us to fashion the world anew in love.

Each day I awaken,
aware of Your sustaining presence
which holds the planets
and sparks our imaginations.

There is nothing to fear,
   though much to lose.
When we turn away from You,
   we turn away from life.

PSALM 4 *REDUX*

I claim my righteousness in the face of those
who would deny me my right,
who would disparage and dismiss me,
who refuse to see the goodness
in my words and in my being.

I turn to You, good God,
who plant the seeds of insight,
who shape the heart for justice,
who herald a renewed humanity
and a redeemed earth.

Be my strength!
Renew my courage!
Restore my dignity among the people,
that they may listen and believe
that Your purposes may be fulfilled.

Keep a guard on my mouth.
Let not my hurt and anger
destroy the possibility
of peace to come.
Wrap me in a wise and thoughtful silence,
that I may discern the right and the true.

Illumine our shadows,
and make our lives
and our life together
radiant with Your light.

You are our joy;
nothing compares,
not the riches of the ages
nor the accolades of our neighbours.

We rest in You,
our trust secure,
our peace assured.

PSALM 8 *REDUX*

O God,
   how we have maligned and misinterpreted You –
placing ourselves above all creation,
commandeering the helm
   that we might control and use
for our own comfort and convenience.

Forgive us.
And restore us to our senses,
that we might see and sense
and know and love
all that is
and all that can be.

May our reverence for You be manifest
in our reverence for all of life.
May our wakeful listening
penetrate the earth and reach
towards the heavens.
May our bold tenderness
overcome our ignorance
and enable wise action.

For this life is a wonder.
You have gifted us with all we need –
beauty and bounty,
word and wisdom,
courage and companionship.

May we enjoy and employ these gifts
as befits those made in Your image.
May all that we make
mirror Your light and Your love.
May Your Being be known and sung
   throughout the world
   with joy and thanksgiving.

O Lord, who may abide in Your tent?
      (the place of rest)
Who may dwell on Your holy hill?
      (the place of flourishing)

Those who are awake
and live in compassion
and listen for truth,
who do not slander
with their tongue
and refrain
from the doing of evil,

in whose eyes
the wonder of creation
and the strife of living
is ever present,
in whose heart
there is room
for the weak
and the strong,
for joy
and for sorrow,

who walk with integrity,
standing by their oath
even to their detriment,
who do not lend money
at interest

7

and do not seek gain
from their friendships,

who see You in all
and all in You.

Those who do these things
shall live.

True Home, how could I choose another?
Fullness to my emptiness,
   water to my thirst,
   ocean to my raindrop,
   still centre point
     that draws me in
     and knows my name.

Wide Plain, where else would I want to roam?
Astonishing vistas,
   expanding horizons,
   infinite grace,
   room to breathe
     and the risk of love
     in the gift of self.

Trustworthy Way, who else could I follow?
Path well-worn and patient,
   bounding freedom,
   nurturing wisdom,
   fulfilling joy.
     Even stumbling
     is not stumbling to You.
   You lift me tenderly
   and invite me on.

> *Therefore my heart is glad,*
> *and my soul rejoices;*
> *my body also rests secure.*

PSALM 18.1–19 *REDUX*

Saved from sure disaster,
plucked from death's grip,
I marvel at the miracle.
My soul exults in strength
summoned from beyond
now coursing through my veins.

It was as though heavens' angels
swarmed and gathered,
a mighty army.
The earth rumbled,
mountains belched fire,
waves crashed:
all that is holy rose up
in a mighty 'No!'
that sounded 'Yes'
to life.

Resurrection illumines:
our deliverance
is the Holy's delight.

PSALM 19 *REDUX*

Radiant warmth of sun,
sheltering softness of cloud,
bejewelled wonder of night sky,
all testify to a glory
beyond our understanding
and our imagination.
A delicate balance of tensions,
a symphony with strength and give,
Being, intricate and breathing,
permeates all, holds all, is all.

We struggle and strive
to read You,
to hear Your melodies
and hum in harmony.
Your song infiltrates our dreams
and shadows our wakefulness.
We are never away from You.
Never.

You are more than we can imagine.
Our knowledge holds You
like mirror shards catching sunlight,
catching starlight, catching candlelight.

You are perfection, completeness, wholeness.
You are past, present, future –
    eternity in a breath,
    infinity in a moment.

You grant us to make our world
with the stuff of Your dreams.
You put strength in our hands
and resilience in our backs.
Before us lies the ancient Way,
    bespoken Wisdom,
    enfleshed Hope,
    courageous Love.
Your light leads us on.

Keep us from arrogance and vanity.
Root our desire in Your goodness
and Your sweet grace.

May our thoughts, our words and our deeds
be worthy of the name You have given us,
the name that gives us life.
Amen.

PSALM 23 *REDUX*

This I know:
My life is in Your hands.
I have nothing to fear.

I stop,
breathe,
listen.

Beneath the whirl of what is
is a deep down quiet place.
You beckon me to tarry there.

This is the place
where unnamed hungers
are fed, the place
of clear water,
refreshment.

My senses stilled,
I drink deeply,
at home
in timeless territory.

In peril, I remember:
Death's dark vale holds no menace.
I lean into You;
Your eternal presence comforts me.
I am held tenderly.

In the midst of all that troubles,
that threatens and diminishes,
You set abundance before me.
You lift my head; my vision clears.
The blessing cup overflows.

This I know:
You are my home and my hope,
my strength and my solace,
and so shall You ever be.

You are my Source, my Way, my Home.
In You I rest secure.
In You I gather strength.
In You I begin to see.

When fear arises
   from within or from without
I remember
   who You are
   and how I am
   in You.

Oh that I may dwell in You
   day by day, moment by moment.
Then peace would be mine.
Then I could persevere
when the waters threaten to overwhelm.
Then my eyes would be filled with beauty
   and my mouth with song.
Then courage and wisdom
would carry me to safe shores.

This I know:
You are.
In You,
I am.

Your goodness is seen
  in the land of the living.
All who turn to You,
  turn towards Home.

PSALM 28 *REDUX*

I seek You
    in silence and in song
    in the faces of strangers
    and the kindness of friends.
Your hiddenness pulls me towards
    what?
You draw me more deeply into life,
    with its hard edges and soft falls,
    its greening and its dying.

Sometimes I am consumed with rage
and rail at injustice.
Is it You overturning the tables?
Or my own hurt reflected and erupting?

It is peace I seek,
and the ability to show mercy,
even as I struggle for justice.

And it is peace You grant.
A strong peace,
rooted at the centre,
a calm and a knowing peace,
a peace that cradles unknowing
    as one would cup a rose
    in one's hand.

Speak of God, children of the Holy:
Speak of God's glory and strength.
Tell of the power of the Name,
   of Word that creates
   of Light that enlivens,
   of Love that binds and frees.
Worship God in radiant splendour,
Worship God in shrouded darkness.
Worship God.

Worship God
   Whose voice storms the waves and stills them,
   Whose whispers shake the living and raise the dead.
Worship God
   Whose shouts shatter fear and explode deafness
   Whose songs echo the soul's deep longing
     and feed the hungry heart.

Worship God
   Whose justice summons the nations,
   Whose mercy lifts the lowly.
Worship God
   Whose silence speaks louder
     than any word that can be said.

Worship God.
Tell of God's glory and power.

Pray for strength.
Pray for blessing.

Blessed are we who seek to know the whole
of who we are:

The gifts	The limits
The light	The shadows
The strengths	The weaknesses
The saint	The sinner

Who know, accept and seek to live in truth,
Who readily say 'I'm sorry' and learn from mistakes,
Who seek the good for all creatures
in the finitude of possibility.

For the weight of harm caused
bears down heavily.
The heart so burdened
cannot sing.
Strength is sapped,
the will paralysed.

Only truth sets us free,
truth and forgiveness,
the deep and gentle acceptance of condition,
the slate wiped clean
to permit love to be writ anew.

Let all burdened seek truth and freedom,
attend to the consequences of choices,
extend and accept the balm of forgiveness,
and face into the future with hope.
Love is come again.

In the depths of silence
and the words of the wise,
our hearts are instructed.
This is the invitation; heed it well.
For torment need not be our lot.
Trust in steadfast love
and the power that moves in all things
to give life.

Be glad and rejoice.
Love is come again,
and again,
forever.

Sing aloud the song of your soul.
Riff the melody that is yours.
Let the life that wells up
erupt in joy and praise:
   L'chaim!   To life!

Sing aloud the song of the earth.
Hum in harmony the tune that holds all.
Let the love that orders existence
exult from your lips:
   L'amour!   To love!

Feel the breath that invites freedom,
   the pulse that sparks creation,
     the contours that call forth justice.

Know the firm faithfulness that inheres.
See the golden cord that gently
   sets the bounds and cradles
   innovation.

Be aware.
Much of what we trust is ephemeral,
malnourished exhalation,
a figment of our illusion.

The way of wisdom counsels humility.
Terra firma is the patient
exercise of hope,
an awakened eye
and an ear tuned to the Holy.

PSALM 34 *REDUX*

May my praise never end.
May the song of my soul
be ever grateful.

For I have known You.
In turning to You,
heart and hands open,
You have met me with grace
and released me from fear.

In Your presence, I stand tall.
I am known and I know.
Clarity and truth well up from within;
I cannot be moved.

My soul magnifies You,
joining the chorus of Mary in the great congregation.
The swell of our voices shakes the foundations.
We have tasted and we have seen.
We have heard and we have hearkened.
Your word lifts and enlivens.
Your power reveals and rescues.
Reverence for You is the beginning of wisdom.

Teach Your children. Remind Your elders.
Share the stories of the goodness and grace of God.
Show the way of seeking and of finding,
of asking and of receiving,
of being blessed to be a blessing.

Speak with humility and gentleness
words of truth and kindness.
Dwell in peace; the Holy is near.

Keep faith.
The trusting heart reaps as it sows:
Life in abundance
and joy made complete.

PSALM 35 *REDUX*

Opposition arises.
Rejection snarls.
Knees shake;
Confidence quakes.

In the face of malice,
    in word and in deed,
I am dumb.

I turn to You,
Defender of the Weak,
You who raise the lame to stand
and cause the blind to see;
You who know my earnest heart,
the good I have done
and the right I have striven for.

The merciless laugh at my stumbling;
my weakness draws wolves
hungry for blood.

Arise, Holy One.
Come to my aid.
Silence my enemies.
Raise me to stand.

Then I will praise You
in the great congregation.
Then Your name will linger on my tongue
as the taste of honey,
the sound of justice.

The solipsistic self
whose heart is turned in on itself,
whose eyes are greedy,
whose hands grasp for gain:
Evil is born here; wickedness broods.
No thought for another;
no knowledge of its own best.
Blinded by envy,
eviscerated by hunger,
bound and boxed,
the will has lost its Way.
Wisdom dissipates
in the face of delusion;
holiness is hidden.

Yet God is.
From dawn through dusk and into the night,
the eternal power we know as love does not fail.
It reveals the poverty of greed
and the possibility of life renewed.
Its ceaseless power is like waves on the sea,
its enduring might like the majesty of mountains;
no act of man or woman can defeat it.

The soul aligned with the power of love
will be satisfied.
Delight in the Holy will fill her mouth
with songs of praise and thanksgiving.
She will build tents to shelter all who seek refuge;

she will set the table for the abundant feast.
All shall drink from the river of life.

O let me dance the dance of life,
let me sing the enduring melody.
Let not wickedness steal my soul.
Let my heart meet evil
with wise compassion.

PSALM 37 *REDUX*

This is the promise:
awakened and patient love
leads to life abundant.

Envy not the prosperity
of the greedy and self-centred.
Self-satisfaction is shallow.
Moth and rust consume treasure.
The heart shrinks as wealth grows;
'enough' eludes.
Grief comes to the rich and the poor,
but joy escapes the grasp
of those who put their trust in riches.

Turn instead towards the Source.
Place your trust in the Eternal.
Persevere in doing right;
delight in dependence on friends.
Give generously.
Share gratefully.
Rest in the evening
with ease.

The years pass.
One seldom sees the fruits of one's labours;
seeds sown produce a harvest uncounted
by the hand of the sower.
Give thanks for the sowing
without thought for the harvest.

In times of sorrow,
accept consolation.
Peace is not far off.
In times of travail,
wait patiently.
Strength for the day will come.
In times of struggle,
wrestle whole-heartedly.
Prayer is heard.

Listen.
Those who turn their hearts toward the Holy
are not disappointed.
Contentment is theirs.
In simplicity is wisdom and peace.

PSALM 40 *REDUX*

I quiet my worried, despairing heart
    and I wait.
The Holy draws near.
I feel myself drawn to a single point;
all of life collapses into a timeless moment.

(I breathe.)

Desolation dissipates.
When I arise, I stand on solid ground.
My self recollected, a song of praise
    erupts from my throat,
    a new song, born of heaven and rooted in earth.
A song of joy. A song of gratitude.

Happy are we who find ourselves in God,
who wait and listen,
who set aside distraction
and see behind the surface satisfactions.
Nothing can compare with the eternal glimmer,
with the whole held in tender hands.
Depths and heights clasp glory;
a whisper of wonder binds all in all.

An opened heart is the divine desire,
not thoughtless obeisance.
Attentive presence is all I have to give
and all You want.
I open the book of my days
that You may write Your story

in the lines of my life.
The flow of ink is smooth and pleasing;
even sorrow and disappointment reveal
the goodness of Your guiding hand.
You have become my delight,
as it is meant to be.

May my testimony ring true
in the ears that hear it.
May my song strike joy
in the hearts of those who catch the harmonies.
May my flesh-made-Word be seen
to reveal Your purpose:
the blessing of all that lives.

Mercy abounds, steadfast love uplifts
and justice springs up where the faithful walk.
I stumble;
my heart fails within me.
I remember:
Your grace saves me.
Nothing can separate
the heart turned Godward
from her salvation.
Again I turn:
You are life and breath to me.
My back toward those
who would denigrate and dismiss me,
I grasp Your goodness with both hands
and pledge my loyalty and my love.

May all who seek You find You.
May all who love You sing You.

As for me, in my weakness and my need,
give me the patience of overwintering seed,
that I may quiet my restless heart,
turn,
wait,
and prepare to receive You.

PSALM 45 *REDUX*

Epiphany
Light of Incarnation:
Human flesh the site
of holy hope
and generous grace.

My heart sings at the beauty
of countless points of light
of every hue and size,
flickering, shimmering,
dancing across the globe.

Light undimmed by travail
and strengthened by challenge,
the light of those gone before still shining,
casting their golden glow over hill and vale,
across oceans and deserts.
Glimmering glances of eternity,
hints and whispers of possibility,
they are invitations to shine,
to come out from under the bushel
and blaze.

Fleshly light reflecting
the Light which gives us life
leads us Home.

PSALM 46 *REDUX*

Sheltering God,
I hide myself in You.
Head swathed and bowed,
I listen for the still, small voice.

Strengthening God,
in times of tumult and terror,
as the earth moves
and the horizon shifts,
You call me back,
to shelter and to strengthen.

Your song is in the sighing of trees.
Your light is in flicker and spark,
knowing and unknowing.
Your power is in the greening,
and in its passing.

Those with ears to hear, listen.
Those with eyes to see, look.

War and peace,
trembling and tenderness,
all that we create
and all that we destroy
hold a holiness
we do not understand.

Illumine our being,
that our doing
might manifest You.

PSALM 47 *REDUX*

May my joy in You never be at the expense of others.
May my neighbours' well-being be to me as my own.
May Your sovereignty be known not by violence,
but in peace secured by justice,
hope undimmed by suffering.

Examine my heart,
and remove all that prevents compassion:
arrogance, fear, greed.

Enlighten my understanding,
and give me all that makes for discernment:
wisdom, patience, kindness.

Enliven my imagination,
and inspire the gifts that bless:
generosity, courage, creativity.

Even as You know us,
make Yourself known through us.
Amen.

The depth of my suffering
in the knowledge of what I have done
is beyond my capacity to speak it,
beyond my capacity to bear it.
I cry out to the Beyond: Have mercy!
Remember my frailty
and the curse of my freedom.
Remember as a Mother remembers
the child whom she has borne.
Remember, and remind me
of the steadfast sureness of Your love.
Remember, and lift me into Your embrace.
Be as balm to me and as bath;
tenderly wash and restore me.
Grant me newness of life.

You awaken me to truth in my inner being.
I enter Your vast silence and listen:
the wisdom of deep structures murmurs.
You hold all contradictions and ambiguities
as though they are but feathers on the wind.
My significance collapses and emerges.

You speak to my deep needs:
to be forgiven,
to be known and still loved,
to be freed to begin again,
to live content, in joy and hope.
In You is life.

Create in me a clean heart,
and put a new and right spirit within me,
as only You can.
And I shall never stop praising You.
I shall seek to speak words that reveal You.
I shall lift my voice and sing of Your salvation.

May Your goodness ever flow among people,
and Your purposes be fulfilled on the earth.

I am under siege.
Criticised, dismissed,
derogated, threatened,
rejected, pressed down.
The enemy once outwith
is now within.
How can I stand?
Strength sapped,
knees weak,
hands tremble.
I am afraid,
afraid for my life.

I turn to You,
Rock of Ages,
Wellspring of Life;
in You I put my trust.
Fear dissipates.
I stand.
Integrity in my right hand,
Love in my left.
Who can defeat me?

Let them assail me.
Let them conspire in dark corners
and watch behind curtains.
Give them their due.
Let the light reveal their wrongs.

Your tenderness enfolds me now,
Your knowing presence
that has seen my struggle
and counted my tears.

I know You are for me
and for life abundant for all.
In You I put my trust.
I stand.
Integrity in my right hand,
Love in my left.
No mortal act,
not even death,
can defeat the eternal power
that courses through the earth
singing justice and
stirring compassion.

My heart is filled with praise.
I lift the blessing cup.
You deliver us
from fear and death,
and place our feet
on the Way everlasting.

PSALM 62 *REDUX*

For You alone my soul waits in silence,
You, my home and my hope.
In You, I rest secure.
Drawing from Your deep well,
I am strengthened.

In the face of the derisive sneer,
the dismissive outburst,
the thoughtless jab,
the blank stare,
I stand still,
listening for kernels of truth,
separating wheat from chaff.

The core of my being is firm and gentle –
I know who I am.
There is room in me to love the unlovely,
to ponder slings and arrows
without retribution,
to remain quiet when there is nothing to say
and to speak when it is time to speak.

The whole of my being
is held in Your steady hands.
I have nothing to fear,
and everything to learn.

So it is for we who trust,
we who wait in silence.

The waiting is a revealing.
The eye sees the folly in vain chasing
after power, wealth and privilege.
The mind notes the clutch and cling
of insecure humanity.
The heart seeks to pledge, saying:
As for me, I want to be a blessing
to heaven and on earth.

Once God has spoken,
twice I have heard:
Love is found in want and in waiting;
the Holy draws us in
and strengthens us to stand.

PSALM 63 *REDUX*

My heart longs for the depths,
for the soul satisfaction
of plumbing the Real
and the Holy.

My breath seeks its Source,
the full inhale
that awakens
and enlivens.

A still sanctuary draws me
towards You,
Source and Silence,
Welcome and Wellspring,
Love and Life.

I tarry here,
my limbs relax,
my core expands
to hold
and be held
by You.

I am held
and I am helped.
I lift my head,
my vision clears.

A song of joy erupts from my being,
breath carries praise
from the depths to the heights,
joining the song of the universe
which is love.

Understanding grows,
granting wisdom in the night
and strength for the day.

PSALM 65 REDUX

Listen!
There is a call to worship
in the hidden sinews
of our being,
a taut string waiting to be plucked,
a melody longing to be sung.

We are made for praise!
An abundant earth calls it forth:
pounding sea and babbling brook,
sighing trees and their singing residents,
shimmering stars and silent night,
the growing and the greening
and the resting seed
invite a joyful song.

A heart freed sings praise!
Surprise of mercy and resonant flesh,
delight tickled, joy unleashed,
tender touch and shared walk,
we shout and sing together for joy.

The whole earth sings praise!
Wild wind whips glory,
babbling brook skipping sings,
green fields davening sway.
The smallest ears pick up the tune
that pulses through all things.

Oh God, Maker of all,
let my life move with
the earth songs beneath my feet
and the star songs above my head.
Let my heart jig and caper like a young lamb.
Let my soul sing and sigh and signify.

No corner of the earth is apart from Your power.
Everywhere a woman may roam,
she will see the signs and hear the songs:
Each day a new day.
Each moment an opportunity.
Each step,
each listening step,
a step in hope's direction.

How may I live my gratitude,
but with humble attention,
with an ear quick to listen,
   gaze penetrating to see,
   a heart ready to love,
   hands eager to bless,

with a mind slow to judge
and probing to discern,
with feet that move
in hope's direction,
dancing earthstar
songs of praise.

So be it.

PSALM 71 *REDUX*

Rescue, Refuge, Rock, Reviver

Rescue
To You, I call
trusting Your ear is tuned
to all You love.
Your firm hand
pulls me out
of crashing waves.

Refuge
In You, I hide
seeking the repose I find
nowhere else.
Your strong silence
anchors me
in storming seas.

Rock
On You, I stand
finding my feet
on terra firma.
Your clear horizon
orients me
to renewing hope.

Reviver
In You, I breathe
fresh, crisp air

tinged with incense.
Your siren song
calls forth
my echoing praise.

Let all the generations know,
   hope,
      and trust.

Sometimes, I lose my way.
I see the fortunes of others,
their supposed ease of living,
their more than enough
with much to spare,
and I envy them.

I forget my own blessings.
I forget that life for all is a struggle.
I forget the poison of too much.
But most of all,
I forget myself,
my true self:
my joy in simplicity and sharing,
the peace of knowing
enough is enough.

Sometimes, a different envy arises.
Gifts of art and music unimaginable to me,
a thick mane of wavy hair,
sleek physique,
rude good health,
the privilege of masculinity.
A veil comes over my eyes.

I wonder at my greed –
why I want all gifts.
I wonder at my vanity
and my vacuity.
For I am gift enough

and my body is mine
to love and to share.
Acceptance settles
more easily into my soul.

You, True North, speak to me in this way.
My compass is set to You.
The desires of my heart are met in You.
In You is fullness of life.

PSALM 80 *REDUX*

I look to the heavens –
longing for the assured ease
of a Saviour who acts apart from us,
who hears our cries and responds,
whose mighty hand rescues and delivers us
even from ourselves.

That God died for me long ago.
I shuffle my way towards the coffin –
reluctant to spade
the last shovelful of earth
into the grave.

Your true power, Holy One,
confounds.
I feel my way towards You.
I breathe Your freshness in the breaking day
and melt into Your comfort at evening's end.
I trace Your contours in the aged lines
of the faces of the long faithful,
and smell You on the tops of infant heads.
I line You in the poetry of ancient texts
and the longings of my heart.

You are.
Of that I am certain.
You alert and invite and wrestle.
You knead us like clay,
Your hands within and outwith
gently moulding.

Do You
– whose imperceptible and patient power
never forces –
do You rescue the unwilling?
Does our summoning cry unlock the mystery
for a moment to allow the flow of You?
Is our awakening an essential prevenience
to Your unleashing?

The responsibility seems light.
You ask no shouldering of the whole,
only a longing heart,
a searching cry,
a hopeful gaze,
a hand open,
willing to be the site
where love may be born.

I look to the heavens –
reports of Your death are exaggerated.
Your ear is keyed to our cry,
Your love hearkened by our longing,
Your power and Your presence
an eternal possibility.

Gratefully, I kneel,
open my hands,
relinquish my fear,
and present myself.

Let Your peace rest on me.
Let Your purposes be made manifest in me.

PSALM 80A *REDUX*

Hear us!
You who are said to hear the cries of the people.
You who hold all time and all matter in Your hands.
You who knelt in the dust to make and to mould us.
Hear and heed. Come, save us!

Bring us to our senses.
Kindle the flame of love within us
that we may live.

Abandoned and lost,
we struggle and strive to no avail.
Puppets with strings cut,
our dance is limp and aimless.
Tears pool around bent ankles.

Bring us to our senses.
Kindle the flame of hope within us
that we may live.

We remember:
it was You who made us,
who formed and fed us,
who liberated and led us.
There was a time
when laughter filled our days
and contentment blessed our nights.
Hand in hand,
we laboured together

in sun and rain.
Joy and gratitude
spilled from our lips.
Purpose and peace
made light work.
All was well.

Turn Your face towards us,
    God of our mothers and our fathers,
    God of our grandchildren,
    God of all that walks, swims or flies
    upon the earth.

Bring us to our senses.
Kindle the flame of faith within us
that we may live.

PSALM 84 *REDUX*

How beautiful, how bountiful is the earth!
How astounding, how awesome are the heavens!
As far as the eye can see and beyond,
    by telescope and microscope,
creation's glory expands the heart in wonder.

The scent of a rose in an overgrown garden seduces.
Gigantic orange poppies with purple-black centres
        stun.
The surround-sound of birdsong uplifts.
The dance of butterflies around buddleia tickles.
Even the prick of the bramble delights,
promising sun-warmed blackberry juice
at summer's end.

This is our home – through soil and sun,
    a miracle of multiplying, evolving cells.
This *is* our home – as much a part of us
    as we are of our parents and of our children.
This is *our* home – ours to know and to love,
    to cherish, protect and behold.
This is our *home* – and it is more glorious
than we can know.
Our home, the dwelling place of muskrats and
        marmots,
kingfishers and kittiwakes, sunfish and sharks.
Our home, where abides the holy and unholy,
chaos and creativity, and the living, dying,
resurrecting eternality of now.

I fall to my knees in thanksgiving and praise.
May my eyes ever be open to Your splendour.
May my ears ever be tuned
to the pulse of life and the song of stars.
May my heart ever be receptive
to the real and the holy within it –
in pain and sorrow,
in plenty and want,
in joy and gratitude.

And where Your people gather
to remember and recollect,
to give thanks and to respond,
to be called to awaken
to being blessed and a blessing,
There, O God, may I serve.
Hands open and lifted,
welcoming song and silence,
willing to be filled, moulded and used.
There I would open the door
to all who seek You
and all who long to sing You.
There I will offer my paltry gifts
for the unending renewal of the human spirit,
the great flow of Your love
in all and through all.

PSALM 89.1–18 *REDUX*

Enduring melody,
Your song shall be sung
so long as the earth spins
and the heavens dance.

Frail flesh opens its mouth:
You are born again.

To songweavers
You are the scale and the tone.
To storytellers
You are the plot and the end.
To all of life
You are breath
and You are beauty.

Open my mouth
and my voice shall rise in praise.

Awaken me, O Lord, from false understanding.
Keep the limits of my knowing ever before me,
that I might not defame You
or claim too much for myself.
Show me true justice and right mercy,
that I may live humbly and simply
in accordance with the order You ordained
for the flourishing of life.

Then my song shall ring with clarion joy,
a call to worship,
an invitation to sing.

PSALM 90 *REDUX*

I stand beneath a canopy of stars and marvel –
   If all time were held in this graced movement,
   If every story began in the swirl
     of dust and gas that shimmers,
Still You would be greater.

I kneel beside a hoed garden bed, head covered –
   If all beauty coalesced in the soft petals of this rose,
   If its scent captured the prayers
     of countless pilgrims,
Still You would be more beautiful.

I hold my lover in my arms, my breath
   a thanksgiving –
   If all human longing were satisfied in this,
   If all tenderness and all courage were born here,
Still Your love would be larger.

Our lives are so small,
yet their drama is writ large:
a slender reed reaches
into the earth for nourishment
and up to the sky for warmth,
vulnerable to drought and flood,
so easily crushed,
so elegantly bowed
by the evening breeze.

We would be beautiful in Your sight,
should You glance this way.
Again from Your lips would we hear
It is very good, indeed.

Bless, O Lord, our immense fragility.
Kiss our bowed heads
and take our shaking hands in Yours.
Lift our eyes towards Your beauty,
and make us to stand
as those who know their own.

The voice is an instrument of joy and blessing:
  a morning song greets the day,
  in the evening a lullaby summons sleep.

Moment by moment, a melody of praise
  – born in the heart –
spills from the lips of the beloved.
The goodness of God,
the power that brought forth the earth
and all that is upon it,
calls forth songs of grateful praise.
The symphony of the spheres
resonates throughout the body.

Even the simple hear and know
the sound of Home.
Only the arrogant,
  whose ears are filled
  with self-congratulation,
miss the music
and the meaning.
They stumble and fall,
their hunger sharpens.

O God of Life:
Let these humble ears hear
the song that hails the new creation.
Let these searching eyes see
the fulfilment of love in this place.
Let these veined hands and this weary back

know their strength and move with grace.
Let these hopeful lips sing Your praise
from the opening of the day
until my last breath.

PSALM 96 REDUX

I open my mouth –
Praise takes flight
like a bird on the wing,
soaring, gliding,
fearless, free.

This new day,
this glorious revelation
of sky and cloud, earth and green,
this gift,
this wondrous gift.

Earth and heaven have cradled this song.
Sunlight and starlight have bathed it;
loam and rock, peat and marsh
structure footfall;
ocean and river, stream and pool
crescendo and trickle,
here, a stop:
breath sheltered by mountains.

A dawn chorus prelude is drawn
from the stillness of dewfall.
The lengthening rays of sun summon
croaking, yelping, mewling, rutting life.
Warmth coaxes seedlings from soil;
leaves stretch and bow towards source;
field and fruits suckle and ripen.

And me. I am ripening too.
Holy hands cup beauty;
wonder opens Way.
This song, my life, an offering
made gratefully, made hopefully, made joyfully.

Earthed in heaven, the heart sings its way Home.

PSALM 97 *REDUX*

Wind and wave and tumult of storm;
earthquake and eruption and torrent of fire;
flood and famine and terror of night;
none of these
equals the power
that spoke matter into being,
aligning the galaxies
and setting the bounds.

Marvel of heavens and fecundity of earth;
seasons and starlight and seedlings and sound;
tenderness of touch and kindness of care;
all of these
testify to the goodness
that wills life,
inviting creation,
opening Way,

calling forth the heart's
silent wonder
and grateful song.

Psalm 98 *redux*

Sing aloud for joy!
Conjure magnificent melodies!
Create meteoritic metaphors!
Reach for the heights of beauty
and the depths of drama!
Use everything to hand –
all that you can make
and all that you can imagine:
stardust and earthdreams,
the music of the spheres
and the mumur of silence,
the hunger of the heart
and the hope everlasting.

The Power within and beyond,
the Presence throughout,
the Wonder and the Glory
call for nothing less
than the full expression
of all that we are
and all that we have.

There is no place
on earth or in the heavens
that has not been soaked in,
tickled or teased by Divine Love.

There is no living creature
on earth or in the heavens

that has not been marked,
grazed or embraced by the Divine Kiss.

There is no song
too lowly or too grand
to offer in praise
and thanksgiving.

Bring your instruments:
blow your horns,
strum your strings,
pound your pianos,
lift Your voices.

Match the roar of the oceans
and the majesty of the mountains.
Let all things magnify Holy might.
Let all things reflect Holy light.

Nothing is apart from,
and all is a part of,
God
whose immensity,
mercy and justice
are forever.

Bless God, O my soul,
and all that is within me,
bless the breath that is life.

Bless God, O my soul,
and remember your awakening
to the power that frees,
the love that reconciles,
the touch that heals,
the mercy that consoles,
the good that uplifts,
the justice that satisfies
    the deepest longing.

History sings Her story
    of Way made known,
    Ground of Being revealed.
Though we see through a glass dimly,
the spark cannot be shrouded.
Her contours are comely.
Our hearts skip a beat, recognising
what our eyes have longed to see:
the goodness of God
in the land of the living.

From everlasting to everlasting,
    God is.
Our time is brief.
From our startled awakening

until the day we return Home,
   we walk in wonder.
Beauty and bounty meet waste and want;
praise and pain keep a tender balance
   (if we are lucky).
The heart knows:
All of life is holy.

So let us live to bless:
Bless the earth and each other,
bless the rain and the sun,
bless the broken-hearted and the hungry,
bless the singer and the song,
bless the seeking and the finding,
bless in living and in dying.
Bless.

Praise God, oh my soul.
The wonder of all creation calls forth praise.
The marvel of the heavens,
   stars flung into space by night,
   cotton candy clouds on a canvas of blue by day,
source of light and life, rain and snow,
wind whipping, cleansing
   making music among the trees.

The solidity and strength of the earth,
   majesty of mountains,
   verdance of valleys,
   dancing deserts and singing streams,
inviting renewal and re-creation
day by day, year to year.

All are at home in creation,
   from the microbe and the mite
   to the elephant and the blue whale.
Trees shelter birds,
seas sustain fish,
every animal has a dwelling place.
Streams tumble down hillsides
and springs bubble up from below;
grasses emerge from soil and fruit from trees.
Watered and fed, we flourish.

The rhythm of days and seasons
orders our work and our rest,
cradling our creativity.

Yet still we struggle.
Made in Your image,
we fashion a world in freedom –
    for good and for ill.
Our generosity pales;
our compassion fails.
In the midst of earth's beauty and bounty,
not all have enough to eat,
not all live in safety and security.

We look to You for life
and for the goodness in our souls.
Renew us to wonder.
Lift our eyes to marvel again
at all that You have made.
Whisper our name *Beloved* –
that we might remember
who we are
and to whom we belong.
Raise us to what we can be,
    a source of blessing to all the earth,
    friends of creation and bearers of hope.
Then You may rejoice in us,
as we rejoice in You.

I will sing of Your goodness all my days.
I will seek to magnify You in my being
as long as I shall live.
At the end, I shall abandon myself
entirely into Your kind hands,
and my praise shall be complete.

PSALM 107 *REDUX*

Raise your voice in thanksgiving;
Sing out the goodness of the Holy
whose constancy and grace are forever.
You who have felt the blessing hand,
lift your voice. Do not hesitate;
tell your story.

Lost and found,
entombed and enlightened,
suffering and saved,
captive and freed,
your story gives life.

Some of you wandered aimlessly,
   lost in a maze of contradiction,
   confused by cacophony.
You put your ear to the ground:
you heard the enduring melody.
You set your feet to follow the pulse of life eternal.
The Holy is your song and your salvation.
You who have heard the soul's sounding,
lift your voice;
tell your story.

Some of you were overcome by despair,
   no flicker of light tempted life.
   Thick shadow clouded possibility
   and choked out hope.

You turned your gaze and caught a glimpse:
The Divine flashed, a kingfisher along the riverside.
Your heart skipped a beat. Death's pall dissipated.
The Holy is your hope and your health.
You who have caught a glimpse and risen to meet it,
lift your voice;
tell your story.

Some of you suffered in silence,
   broken in body,
   marred in mind,
   sorrowful in spirit.
'Is there no relief?' you prayed,
'Am I all alone?'
One day, a kind hand took yours and held it.
A listening ear bent low and heard you into speech.
The warmth of love began its healing magic.
The Holy is your comfort and your courage.
You who have felt the tender touch,
lift your voice;
tell your story.

Some of you were bound in chains of steel,
   captive to forces within and outwith,
   struggling against powers too strong,
   flailing against fate and chance.
You stopped, and took a breath.
And another.
Peace flooded your being,
peace and power.
A stronger being flowed into relaxed veins.
A wise agency enabled thoughtful choice.
The Holy is your strength and your solace.

You who have stood by a strength not your own,
lift your voice;
tell your story.

Our limits confound us.
Our vulnerability frightens us.
But to the Holy,
    whose infinite compassion seeks the lost
    and embraces the fearful,
they are but opportunity.

Turn your ears to the enduring melody.
Catch a glimpse of the Divine dancing.
Open a hand to the kind possibility.
Take a breath of peace passing understanding.

The Holy is.
We are not alone.
A greater being desires our well-being
and resources our re-creation.
Love seeks a willing accomplice.
The earth awaits our resurrection.

Raise your voice in thanksgiving.
Sing out the goodness of the Holy
whose constancy and grace are forever.
You who have felt the blessing hand,
lift your voice. Do not hesitate;
tell your story.

PSALM 116 REDUX

Drowning.
Your hand rescued me.
Wounded.
Your balm soothed me.
Terrified.
Your peace encompassed me.
Lost.
You found me.

Your healing love weaves
the tattered pieces of my life
into a garment of joy.

You gave me my life.
How may I repay You but
to live it – joyfully, gratefully,
sharing the love that has made me whole,
singing of Your goodness in the land of the living,
and dying in peace when my time comes
– the Shema on my lips.

You are my God, You alone.

PSALM 119.33–50 *REDUX*

The ancient Way lies before me,
the Way of my mothers and fathers.
It is the Way of Life,
    strong life, courageous life, kind life.
A Way that beholds beauty and welcomes wonder,
a Way that nurtures knowledge and wrestles wisdom,
a Way that fosters freedom and bespeaks blessing.

I seek to follow well-worn paths to new places,
moving by divine pulse and breath,
stopping to give thanks along the Way,
dancing joy and laughing pleasure,
wiping tears and lending strength,
sheltering the vulnerable and feeding the hungry.

This is my great desire,
day by day, and moment by moment,
for Your life, O God, to be
my light and my love for all time.

PSALM 121 *REDUX*

I look to the horizon –
  What will tomorrow bring?
  Today I can scarcely stand.
Who will come to my aid?
How will I survive this?

My eyes are drawn beyond –
  beyond the ruins that lay around me,
  beyond the deep ache that has taken up
  residence within me,
  beyond the limits of my capabilities,
  the weakness of body and mind.

There I find You.
Your stolid peace immoveable
in the vicissitudes.
Your easy breath unimpeded
by our anxious wrangling.
Your gentle Being implacable,
quietly present
before, beneath and beyond.

You at the beginning.
You at the end.
You in the middle.
Always, and everywhere,
You.

Creator and re-creator,
keeper and lover,
shelter and sustainer,
You.

From this time on and forevermore,
I put my trust in You.

When the miracle happened;
when the hoped for, dreamed of,
prayed for, longed for,
ached for, pleaded for
miracle happened;
when You acted beyond
our expectation or imagination,
we were open-mouthed.
We pinched ourselves.
Can it be? Is it true?

Then delight began
in our toes
and rippled its way
to the tops of our heads.
Laughter
and tears
erupted.
We clapped our hands.
We danced with joy.

This is God's doing, we said,
The Holy is.

Even our sceptical neighbours noticed:
Is this God's doing?, they muttered.
Can God save me?, they wondered.

Act again, great God,
with unmistakeable power.

We bring our need to You –
   our poverty of spirit,
   our deep hungers,
   the work of our hands and minds,
   the mistakes we've made,
   the seeds we've sown.

Make our barren places fruitful
and our emptiness to overflow.
Free us from our manifold captivities
and set us on a broad plain.
Fill our mouths with laughter again
and our hearts with songs of joy.

Psalm 127 *redux*

Creating and recreating, energy
weaves and wanders,
ducks and dives.
Singularity flashes,
surfing undulating waves of light;
no flash an island unto itself.
The seen and the unseen,
the part and the whole,
the human and the divine
jitterbug and jive to a tune
set by the One who holds all
in firm and tender hands.

Or is the One the centripetal point?
Outer boundary or inner magnet,
security is in the holding
tension that shelters risk and rest.

These words my offering
to the swirl
and the source.

PSALM 128 *REDUX*

Joyful are those who abide in God,
   whose ears are tuned to the song of the faithful,
   whose eyes behold glimpses of holiness
   in the everyday and the extraordinary.

Grateful are those who know themselves
beloved and blessed,
   who offer a hand to those in need,
   whose gentleness brings calm.

Those gathered around the table of love
will never go hungry.
Happiness will flavour their days;
at night they rest content.
Their kindness feeds the flourishing of others,
as the cup overflowing
slakes the thirst of many.

May the Holy ever bless you in your home.
May your family thrive
and your friendships grow strong.
May we see the reign of justice and joy
in our land and beyond.
May generations to come know peace
and live to praise.

Psalm 130 *redux*

Fear gnaws at my belly.
Despair creeps into my heart.
I stretch my neck towards the sky
and let the anguish escape from my throat.

Hear me!

O God, Merciful and Just,
any scale will find us wanting.
Who can stand before You
without regret?
Without the shame
that bows the head?

I wait.
My hands are empty now.
I cannot save myself.

I wait.
My soul waits;
I dare to hope.
Eyes fixed on the horizon,
breath slow and even,
I wait.

For I know:
You are.
Love is alive;
the greening stirs
in dark loam and will
burst into the light
soon.

PSALM 131 *REDUX*

O Lord, my heart is open
and my mind is freed
from the struggle to make sense
even of who, of how, You are.

  (I breathe.)

I come to the broad plain,
the fullness of silence,
to You.
Peace envelopes me.
I sink into You.
I want for nothing.

  (This is the still point
  of the turning world.)

I rest in You.

  (This is the beginning.
  I am.)

PSALM 133 *REDUX*

Oh how wonderful,
how joyous it is
when we dwell together
in peace and unity.

It is like a good meal,
the satisfaction
of a full belly.

It is like hearty laughter,
cleansing tears,
knowing looks.

It is like the freshness of the morning.
It is like the comfort of nightfall.

Here the Holy blesses,
now and forever.

As close as breath, You are.

The mystery of Your being
   so intimate, so strange.
A silken veil obscuring vision;
a compelling luminescence
that will not be solved.

You are the light and the veil.
You are the weaver and the cloth.
You are the dancer and the dance.

There is nowhere
You are not.
There is nothing
not in You.

All of time and space
cohere in You.
The smallest particle,
   the largest galaxy,
the mite
   and the mammoth
bear Your imprint.

From before conception,
You order our being.
We are a wonder,

a miracle in flesh and blood:
  bodies that bruise and heal,
  minds that grasp and grow,
  hands that care, craft and create.

We reach our limits,
  and there we find You.
We contract to the still centre;
  there You are.

Blessed are those who seek You
and blessed are those who sense You.
Blessed are those who,
catching the light from the corner of their eyes,
turn and face You.
Blessed are the barefoot
and blessed are those who cover their heads.

Blessed are the lips that sigh: *Holy, holy, holy.*

PSALM 141 *REDUX*

This I desire:
    that my heart be set upon Your heart's desire
    that my words make way for Your enfleshed Word
    that my hands proclaim Your love unbounded.

And when I stumble,
    when I forget my belovedness in Your eyes,
    and ignore the belovedness of others,
gently turn me back
to gaze again on Your knowing face
and find myself restored.

Let not riches or the regard of others
distract me from the simplicity and joy
of life in You.

PSALM 145, A CONVERSATION

Stillpoint and Centre,
Wonder and Way,
I praise You.

Eternal Source,
Cohering Power,
Mystery Beyond our Knowing.

What song can I sing
that could capture Your essence?
I am dumb.
Only silence may suffice.

Yet try I must,
that the generations will know,
and the seeking will find
and the finding will live
   with grace and purpose,
   in peace and patience,
   with joy and kindness.

The old words clang,
their resonance lost in time.
Yet the power beneath
remains,
to tease and haunt,
as shackle and lifeline.

This is our conundrum:
To glimpse eternity
in the frail vessels
that are words,
that our own flesh
– equally frail –
may tell the story
of life abundant.

Praise the All –
   the Soil, the Source,
   the Power, the Pulse,
that which surges into life,
sweeping death up into its current.
Praise God!

Praise the All –
   from the heights,
   in the depths,
   in the voice of all things:
crash of waves and rush of wind,
song of bird and roar of lion,
open-throated praise of woman and man.
Praise!

Praise twinkling in the starry night.
Praise rumbling through the stormy sky.
Praise roiling in the deepest sea.
Praise!

Praise in the swirl of electron
   and the chain of DNA.
Praise in the pull of gravity
   and the inertia of stone.
Praise in the nascent bud
   and the flowing stream.
Praise!

Praise in you and praise in me.
Praise in old and praise in young.
Praise in song and praise in story.

All of life sings Praise!

PSALM TO THE THREE-IN-ONE

(meditation on Köder's *Maternal Womb*)

Blessed are You, O Holy One,
  who crowns the earth with beauty,
  who brings forth the greening
    and blesses the dying,
  who summons the songs of the beloved.
Blessed are You.

Blessed are You, O Holy One,
  who absorbs the pain of the world,
  who cradles broken bodies and sorrowful spirits,
  who loves us back to life.
Blessed are You.

Blessed are You, O Holy One,
  who waits in silence,
  who holds the seeds of new life,
  who keeps counsel with the wind.
Blessed are You.

Blessed are You, Three-in-One and One-in-Three,
  whose love holds the universe together
  and binds the human family to dust and stars.
Blessed are You.

PSALMS AND PRAYERS FOR THE MOMENT

MONDAY PRAYERS (FOR BEGINNINGS)

At every beginning,
bless our dreaming
and our doing.

The day (week, month, year) lies before us,
full of the mundane and the miraculous,
the known and the unknown.

Be the breath we take before each step.
Be the source from which we draw strength.
Be the end toward which we direct our hope.

Open our eyes to all that is around us.
Open our ears to the song the soul yearns to sing.
Open our hearts to the love that lives through us.
Open our hands to the task the moment requires.

Let us do this one thing,
the thing before us,
as if all creation
and our very life
depend upon it,

as if You are bent over,
watching and listening
and willing us
to do it well.

Tuesday Prayers (for family and friends)

We pray for those closest to us,
the people whose lives
   by birth and by choice
are intertwined with our own.

We name them . . . . . .

Meet each at their point of need
and lift them in love.
Enable their growth
in wisdom and grace.
Bring each life to the fullness
of joy, purpose and peace
that You desire for all creation.

Where we have failed each other,
   prompt forgiveness.
Where we have harmed each other,
   provide healing.
Where we have blessed each other,
   provoke thanksgiving.

So may we live with one another
in love,
   awake to frailty,
   grateful for grace,
   tender in patience.

Wednesday Prayers (for those in need)

For the hungry and the homeless,
For the heartless and the hopeless,

For the lonely and the longing,
For the overlooked and the unloving,

For the bleeding and the dying,
For the aching and the crying,

For all who need and all who plead,
For the empty hand and the asking heart,

Grant us to see, O Lord, it is You
Who are meeting us.

Thursday Prayers (for religious leaders)

God, in Your grace,
pour out Your Spirit
on those chosen and choosing
to exercise leadership
in churches, synagogues, mosques
and wherever people gather
to seek Your face
and drink deeply from Your well.

Give them sweet humility,
dogged perseverance
and listening ears.

Accompany them through
the hard and confusing places.
Bless their wrestling.
Cradle their courage.
Develop their discernment.
Excite their imagination.
Prosper their efforts.
Strengthen their trust.
Yoke their passion.

Place a sustaining word on their tongues
and a joyful song in their hearts.

At the end of the day,
grant them peace.

Amen.

Friday Prayers (for teachers and learners)

Learning is in our DNA.
When You knelt in the dust
and tenderly, firmly shaped our flesh,
You made us flexible, adaptable,
able to grow and learn
in every environment.

Neural pathways map an information network,
every sense alive and receiving,
the miracle of learning
   (sorting, playing, storing)
continues even while we sleep.

Bless our striving to learn
and to unlearn.
Hone our senses.
Enable our knowing
in body and in mind.
Grow up within us
the wisdom that brings life.

Give teachers
   a listening ear
   a discerning mind
   a wise heart
the courage to welcome the conflict
out of which learning grows
and the patience to accompany
and steer its process.

Give students
   a thirst to know
   a willingness to risk
   a pride in accomplishment
the kindness to welcome the sharing
out of which learning grows
and the patience to try, to fail,
and to try again.

Help us all to learn
the goodness of the earth,
the tenderness of the human heart,
and the blessing we were made to be.

So may we flourish,
as You intend.

Amen.

Saturday Prayers (for the earth)

For this earth,
this good earth,
for the work and life of nematodes,
of worms and woodlice
and all creatures that work the soil.
Thank You for the ground on which we walk,
for its firmness and its fecundity.

For tadpoles that wriggle and sunfish that sparkle,
for all the swimming, skimming, diving life
that fills earth's watery veins and arteries,
for rivers and oceans and lakes and puddles,
for hydrogen and oxygen that marry to slake life's
    thirst.
Thank You for the water from which life emerges
and by which life thrives.

For sunlight and starlight
and the shining of the moon,
for darkness and shadow and earth's subtle turning,
for tides and for seasons,
for the cycling of fallow and fertile.
Thank You for the rhythm of sleeping and waking,
of being and making.

Thank You.

Sabbath Song

Welcome this day,
   this gift,
this jewel
   that crowns all days.

I turn uplifted face and hands
towards the sun
of Your countenance.

I woo You,
that Your languorous ways
might infect and inhabit me,
body and soul.

You are siren song,
summoning me not to crash
upon indifferent rocks,
but to float,
   buoyant,
held up by the ocean
which is the Whole.

My hands stilled,
my mind quietens.
I shed the anxiety that rules the other days
like a snakeskin grown brittle.

The fresh breeze a caress,
   the scent of hyacinth a seduction,
the blue sky never bluer,
   even blades of grass startle.

Time suspends.
Now is enough.
Today is forever.

A January Prayer

For these things,
I give You thanks –
   a warm radiator on a cold day,
   sweet bread and tea in the afternoon,
   a hasty smile, gaze lightly held,
   the stiff breeze that refreshes
   and the fleece that repels it.

For friendship
   that counts the tears
   and shares delight.

For love,
   quiet and steadfast,
   that holds the memory of fire.

My cup, O Lord, truly overflows.
Let me not refuse to bless
when I have been so blessed.
Stretch ever wider my heart,
extend my reach
and anchor our hope.
Amen.

2012, St Beunos

MOTHERING SUNDAY PSALM

You were the first.
You know the power and the pain,
    the melting and the moulding,
    the hopefulness and utter helplessness.

Did Your womb contract fiercely
when You said *Let there be light?*

Did waves of love course
through Your being when
You first saw the earth,
a shining marble of blue and green,
wisps of white clinging,
lit up by moonlight
in the sea of night?

And later, when those You made in Your
image, took their freedom and ran with it –
did You cry Yourself to sleep?
Did fear bring You to Your knees?
Did You wonder what terrible thing
You had unleashed by Your love?

You were the first.
After You, many followed
and many more will.
What future worlds promise or threaten?
Will freedom cost us our lives?

Still You are faithful.
Your tears water our gardens.
Your dreams dog our days.
Your song summons our hope.
Your prayers hold our hearts.

Prayer for the New Year

Be gentle with me, God.
Open the way before me.
Provide refreshment:
clear water, fresh breeze.

Still my anxious, striving mind.
Bind my aching, yearning heart.
Focus my straining, hoping energies.
Accomplish within me what You can.

Give to me
perseverance in work,
direction in darkness,
the strength to stand
and the wisdom to walk
with grace,
that I may feel
the weight
and value
of each step.

Psalm for the Year's End

Here I am.
What is done is done.
What is undone
nourishes seeds still hidden.
Nothing is lost.

Here I am.
A little more hollowed out by grief,
a little wiser for the wear and tear,
my eyes are open now.
There is a dawning knowing in me
of beauty and of terror.
My soul stretches to hold it.

Here I am.
Joy has made a home in me.
Its radiance warms
and extends.

The light shines brighter.
Ancient songs glow
with a wisdom
for which I hunger.

PSALM FOR THE OVERSUBSCRIBED

Pushed to the edge
by forces within and outwith,
I catch my breath.

Stepping back
to recollect in calm,
I labour against the flow
of strong feeling.

Seeking wise counsel,
breathing deeply,
I contemplate consequences.

Surprised by the river of rage
flowing so close to the surface,
I labour to bring a broader perspective.

Diminished by exhaustion,
resentment and rage bubble up
and boil over with little provocation.

A gentle voice calls: Be still.
Drink deeply. Rest surely.
You know the Way.

My hands are open now.
The shore does not fear
the pound of waves,
but welcomes them,
lets them soften
shell and stone
into sand.

SCARBOROUGH PSALM

Waves crash and cleanse.
Larger forces set the movement
   the coming in,
   the going out,
   encroachment,
   recession.

Yet the sea is still the sea,
a unity.
A thing to be trusted:
It is what it is.

Throw away the hammer.
Let planks become driftwood –
   it is their destiny.

Float face up,
   boatless,
   open to sun and rain.
Let the ocean cradle and toss you.
All shall be well.

So much of life
   is spent clutching
   and shaping.
That is good too.

But from time to time
float.
Be borne up.
Trust.

Doing and not doing
   are good.
Listen.
The sea gull's song pierces
a grey sky.

Singing is good.
Silence is good.

Waiting for Resurrection
(for survivors of domestic and church violence)

Countless crucified
wait for resurrection.

Slapped by hands once held
in tender covenant promise.

Cast from communities
whose lips mouthed love,
eyes dulled with indifference.

Bodies and minds scarred
by the failure of love
in deep places.

Butt of jokes,
receptacle for fear,
rejected mirror of vulnerability.

Is it the human condition to
    destroy what we fear,
    become what we hate,
    betray who we are?

Countless crosses litter roadsides,
rocky paths and derelict sites.
No garden tomb, few weeping women, only
bedsits and half-empty houses,
the quiet of a home become prison
broken by the babble streaming

from electric wires, the tangled
illusion of connection
a cold comfort, but
comfort nonetheless.

Waiting for resurrection,
comfort is taken
wherever it can be found.

Waiting for resurrection,
the mind surfs and clings,
words become life rafts,
an image a buoy.

Waiting for resurrection,
endless night hard to bear,
we labour to lift our heads
and strain to see a point of light.

WINDERMERE PRAYER

Mouth to mouth resuscitation

I drag myself dutifully
   to the place
   where prayer had been made valid.
Exhaustion pulls at my limbs
   and tugs my eyelids closed.
'Let us pray' – she says.

I open my mouth
   You come near;
   You are close . . .
   as close as my breath.
I inhale deeply.
I surrender the whole of being
into the Breath.

Again and again, I breathe.
   You are my life support.
   You are the lover whose kiss brings me life.
   You – imperceptible and tender –
      the light buzz of almost
      the quiver of now
      the tickle of desire.

I breathe You.

'Murder the little darlings,'
she said.
She'd picked up that pearl
at a creative writing workshop.
'You'll fall in love with what you write.
You've got to . . .
murder the little darlings.'

The editor's pen is sharper than the sword.
The surgical scalpel threatens to eviscerate
the soul of the sonnet.
Highlight/delete slays thousands
in one fell swoop.

The captivating concept,
so artfully articulated:
will it survive
the daring discernment driven
by the intent of intelligibility?

The heart quakes,
and prays for resurrection.

CPSIA information can be obtained at www.ICGtesting.com
Printed in the USA
LVOW05s0315010714

392365LV00004B/5/P

9 781848 256392